T0162077

RELIQUARIES

RELIQUARIES

Eric Pankey

AUSABLE PRESS
2005

Design and composition by Ausable Press.
The type is Granjon with Charlemagne Titling.
Cover design by Rebecca Soderholm.

PUBLISHED BY
AUSABLE PRESS
1026 HURRICANE ROAD, KEENE NY 12942
www.ausablepress.org

DISTRIBUTED BY
CONSORTIUM BOOK SALES & DISTRIBUTION
1045 WESTGATE DRIVE
SAINT PAUL MN 55114
800-283-3572
FAX: 651-221-0124

The Acknowledgments appear on page 113 and constitute
a continuation of the copyright page.

Library of Congress Cataloging-in-Publication Data
Pankey, Eric, 1959—
Reliquaries / by Eric Pankey. — 1st ed.
p. cm.
ISBN 1-931337-12-8 (pbk. : alk. paper)
1. Brothers—Death—Poetry. 2. Elegiac poetry, American. 3. Grief—Poetry. I. Title.

PS3566.A575R45 2005
813'.54—dc22
2004030345

In memory of my brother
David Arthur Pankey

RELIQUARIES

III.

IV.

Godi se il vento ch'entra nel pomario
vi rimena l'ondata della vita:
qui dove affonda un morto
viluppo di memorie,
orto non era, ma reliquiario.

— Eugenio Montale

I.

LIGHT BY WHICH I READ

One does not turn to the rose for shade, nor the charred song of the
     redwing for solace.
This past I patch with words is a flaw in the silvering,
                                memory seen
     through to.
There I find the shallow autumn waters, the three stolen pears,
The horizon edged with chalk, loose where the fabric frayed.
Each yesterday glacier-scored, each a dark passage illumined by a
     honeycomb.

I begin to fathom the brittle intricacy of the window's scrim of ice.
For years, I managed without memory—stalled, unnumbered,
     abridged—
No more alive than a dismembered saint enthroned in two hundred
     reliquaries.
Now, it is hard not to say *I remember,*
                         hard, in fact, not to remember.
Now, I hear the filament's quiver, its annoying high frequency, light
     by which I read.

River mist, mudbanks, and rushes mediate the dark matter
Between two tomorrows:
                        one an archive of chance effects,
The other a necropolis of momentary appearances and sensations.
One, a stain of green, where a second wash bleeds into the first.
The other time-bound, fecund, slick with early rain.

✳

As if to impose a final hermeneutic, all at once the cicadas wind down.
The gooseberry bush looms like a moon: each berry taut, sour, aglow.
The creek runs tar in the cloud-light, mercury at dusk.
Then the frogs start up.
                        Clay-cold at the marrow. A hollow pulse-tick.
And it seems, at last, I've shed my scorched and papery husk.

OWL IN THE VINEYARD

Thought after thought the wheel turns: desire, form, formlessness,
And there beyond no-thought, desire.
                                        I listen to the crows
Dicker as they gather in the canopy of a narrow tract of woods.
I consult almanacs and star charts.
I put a stick through the spokes, but it does not stop the headlong
        turning.

One must catch the scent of the wolf before it catches one's own,
Which is to say, the wind is a variable, and never a constant:
The wind warped by the cedar; wind clenched in embers;
The wind like a midday trance as the horizon is swallowed by a snake.
How does the bee ride the poppy in a sun-struck field of wind?

I say a prayer for the world and in the midst lose my place
Amid the winter garden, the rain garden,
                                        the minor chord of seasons.
With grassfire cinders, I smudge in the blur between sky and water,
Re-inscribe the coordinates of the unmarked mass graves, the road
        into the forest.
Daily, anonymity and vanity escort me home. Daily, I say my prayers.

Lead gives back little light and what it gives it does so miserly,
Sullenly, with an exhausted shrug, neither a bribe nor a tribute.
There are times when the fire is mineral and the wind is mineral.
There are times when I say *I* when I mean everything I am not:
An owl in a vineyard, say, or an unrepentant exile.

THE FEVER AND THE DREAM

The tide-wash draws itself thin across the marsh surface,
The light dappled and depleted, porous and vestigial.
I am an archivist of light effects, each offered as an *ex-voto,* a sacrifice,
A stand-in for all I will not allow myself to say.
                                        Whose pruning hook
Cleft the devil's hooves? Whittled the moon to a sickle?

I look in on paradise through a peephole: the ditch a clot of weeds,
The nuthatch pestering a paste of seeds lodged in pine bark,
The black snake, a slip of breath and spark,
                                        coiled in the cut-back roses.
To minimize disappointment, one follows the magician's misdirection,
Refuses to see the performance for just what it is and has been: a trick.

Asked to define the moment, I offered the following: a preserve,
        a theater,
An enclosure, a habitat, a dossier, a drawer for souvenirs, a curio
        cabinet,
A vestibule, an apparition in a bell jar. Luckily, there were no follow-
        up questions.
In each moment, I see the lightning trace of the Maker's hand.
                                        Or to
        embellish:
The lightning trace of the Maker's hand separating day and night.

I always longed for an ear like that: to hear the locks, one by one,
      tumble and release.
Hans Bellmer said, "Desire shapes the image of the desired one."
Cold Mountain admonishes, "If pleasures come be happy."

                                       I put my
      hands over my ears,
Shut my eyes, hum to keep myself from thinking, yet the fever and
      dream persist:
The fever a whetstone, the dream a honed ax-edge.

TOKEN OF THE SACRED

Beneath the earth, coal is ablaze, coal smolders, mute matter in
       translation.
Oats loosed by wind lift, tumble, and settle in a random elsewhere of
       a shallow depression.
The moon tugs at my bones,
                    yet I argue for the rare and mystical
       world of the spirit.
Daedelus made practical order of the maze when he crafted his final
       work, a golden honeycomb.
Milk and honey we imagine in paradise, sweetness and sweetness to
       cut the bitter.

The page—foxed, stained with snowflakes, dog-eared for quick
       reference—
Holds on by threads. The chapter titled: "The Floating World (Act II),"
The chapter subtitled: *"In which the god's indifference is figured as drawn
       axes and curves,*
Parabolas, cast points upon a plane, and not, as I had expected,
By an empty foyer of wind, by blown-out butter lamps along the hall."

The shuttle slips in and out of the warp, the pattern exposed thread by
       thread.
A thousand bolts of silk and still there is tomorrow to prepare for, to
       fashion,
To reveal at last.
           Good luck, my brother and I would say to our father,
       when luck had not yet run out

At the start of some scheme that would set right all the previous
    failed schemes.
The past is a millstone incised with a flint burin, an inventory of the
    dead.

The mast traces an ellipse of stars, and on clouded nights a cloud-
    covered vacancy.
The water, split by the bow, is like cut flesh, the occult workings
    glimpsed:
Transparence, translucence, opalescence.
                      In a dream, the maze,
    drawn with a stick in sand,
Circumscribes and encloses a token of the sacred and although I
    made the maze myself,
Full of false passages and dead ends, I cannot find my way to the
    center.

REFRAIN

Once more the premise of autumn, the austerities of in-betweenness,
The earth of ether afloat on bedrock as shadows lessen, then draw
      long.
I have made of this body a vacancy and still cannot prove the spirit's
      argument of pure being.
Once more the residuum of leaf-fall. Once more the mutable realm
      of matter displaced.
Once more the shiver and query in the blank but never empty mind
      of the willow.

How palpable, now, that life that once seemed a seeming, a
      miscellany of manageable pain.
The early winter sunlight, cloud-scattered, paltry, is cast like straw on
      a muddy path,
Straw caught on a gust and blown over a ditch of stumps and stalks.
      Sometimes I forget
That I am marking time amid the remnants of the world, a world I
      failed to mourn.
The scree and ice skitter down behind me, twilight and its echo.

Unchecked, the sap oozes from the hacked-back cherry's bark. Pollen
      and spores dust the pavement.
On clear nights, a voluptuary might collate the abductions, betrayals,
      and myths from starlight.
I would not choose to be reborn. I would refrain—

                         meaning *to cease,*

    and not *to repeat.*

My brother is dying. My brother will die. My brother has a year to
    live.
I would refrain. I would refrain meaning *to cease*.

One does not need a scale to know what will and will not balance,
But one measures nonetheless to confirm the known.
To fall asleep, I tried to stay awake. I listened to the cricket, to a
    raindrop or two on the sill,
To my brother's troubled breathing in the next bed, to tornado
    weather in the distance.
I counted my blessings. Enumerated my troubles. I woke to
    morning's heavy, humid air.

THE BACK-STORY

The notebook—benedictions and burlesques, wishes and whatnot—
      is full and closed.
The door, ajar, will slam shut when another door is opened.
                                   So much
      for the confessional mode.
I have three parallel scars that run across my lower back and no
      notion of what caused them.
Uncertain of the when and the why, this is the point where, by
      convention, I look out the window
As if the pine, poplar, holly, dogwood and the gravel-filled creek bed
      below were, in fact, a refuge.

The night-fog was like lampblack on curved glass. I drove down into
      the valley and was covered,
Then up again into tree-laden ghost-dark, the pitch and grainy green
      of the forest.
My eyes closed for an instant. Two deer, stark in the headlights,
      stood, gravity-freighted,
Then flew—apparitions, eidolons, messengers—bright antler-tips
      white gold.
                    My eyes opened
To the shimmy and jar of the shoulder's rumble strip as I plunged
      back down into fog.

I finger each memory as if it were a prayer bead, but each crumbles as
    salt to the touch.
I look at my hands and count a paper-cut, four calluses, a blood
    blister.
           So much for the epic mode.
All day I make offerings to the shades, wrest whatever clues they
    cleave to.
All day I make offerings to the shades, steal what would be given
    freely were I a shade.
When I come home, my dog lifts her head—not to greet me—but
    to confirm I am the one who left.

"I was driving late, and sure I was drunk," George said, drunk and
    animated, as he recalled the story,
"And there he was, huddled in the middle of the road and I couldn't
    stop and the car thudded
Over him. I killed him, no doubt about it, but the police said he had
    been robbed, and beaten-up
And badly, and left there in the middle of the road for dead. I
    finished him off."
           George took consolation
In the back-story, in all that was never in his hands to change for the
    better or the worse.

LET ME REST ON THAT PEACEFUL MOUNTAIN

Soon enough I will wash my hands above the spoils, soon enough
     feast among the flies
At a table, daubed and speckled, where my ghost will sit before the
     body it once burdened.
Until then, I transcribe the changes: salt into air, air into anthracite,
     anthracite into fern.
Until then, I watch the creek shrink and fill through the seasons.
I watch the moon, cloaked in camouflage, lift like a zeppelin.

"Those old songs are my lexicon and prayer book," Dylan says of "I
     Saw the Light,"
"Let Me Rest on that Peaceful Mountain," and "Keep on the Sunny
     Side."
I put on Neil Young's "Only Love Can Break Your Heart," Tom
     Waits' "Jesus Gonna Be Here"
And "The Cold, Cold Ground,"
                    and Emmylou Harris's cover of
     Lucinda Williams' "Sweet Old World."
What comfort I feel, though broken and buried, at the promise of
     redemption on this earth that is passing.

More and more I forget the names of things or I'll step into a room
     and forget why I entered.
If I wait, what has slipped catches up with me, the name or reason,
     and I go about my business.
Every day at 5:05 p.m. someone calls, and when I pick up the phone,
     the person says nothing.

Hello, I say once or twice, then we listen to one another breathe and
      neither of us wants to be the first
To hang up, to be the one to let the other have such a sublime,
      mischievous, and useless satisfaction.

A hawk settled and preened on a low-branched oak outside the
      church window.
I was impatient at that very moment with questions of the spirit.
Pure in its severity, the hawk turned its head, and though I saw its
      eyes, I did not meet them.
Beyond those wooded acres:
                        the Little River Turnpike, the road home.
How often the *out-there* seems a diorama, a lesson in an enclosure, an
      example of the real.

SOMETIME PRIOR

Through the raveled blue of my mother's blown smoke rings,
                                                    I looked
        into the future.
Then as now, the road rolls behind like a winding sheet into a forest
        with Spanish moss.
Then as now, the moon, my one companion, drifts beside me on a
        current of stars.
I'm gonna take a sentimental journey, she sings between drags.
Where we had been I cannot say, half-awake for hours, the wheels'
        thrum unsteady at such speeds.

If the words of scripture are undeceptive, then heaven's edge is this
        trace
Of perfume on the air: autumn white camellias.
Between cradle and crux, the flesh is wed to the bone.
Biding his time,
        Jesus writes with his finger in the dirt.
One cannot help but try to read what is written there, what he wrote
        there biding his time.

There along the path into the woods,
                      I found a mat of leaves and dry
        needles
Beneath the low-slung pines and shade where some animal or person
        had pressed its weight and rested.
Ice and its cognate cold smelled of woodsmoke. Even after the cops
        came

My mother and father argued day and night: accusations, threats,
 curses,
A scrawny script they knew by heart, their performances ravishing
 and spellbinding, flames let loose.

Apparently he had fucked someone else at the party. *Fuck you,* she
 said. *Fuck you,* he replied.
Or perhaps it was before the party, sometime prior, and the someone-
 else was at the party.
I tried not to hear, and yet could not quite decipher all I heard. *Fuck
 me,* she said later. *Fuck me.*
And they were fucking,
 both of them crying out, *Fuck, O Fuck,* the
 word like gristle on my tongue.
I sat at my bedroom window flicking June bugs as they landed on the
 screen, my light on to lure more.

BLIND WILLIE JOHNSON SINGS

More spits, erupts, and spills from the ingot—splashed embers, little
      solar flares—than fills it,
And when the molten cools in the grim foundry light—dull, graying,
      base—one can almost not see,
Blinded by the viscous afterimage, the heavy liquid haloed, as it dims
      to solidity.
Each story of metamorphosis builds into its equation the cost of such
      elaborate transformation.
This is not *that,* although in the stories one tells *this* is always *that,*
      the same, the same yet *this.* Yet *that.*

I filled the wheelbarrow with cordwood the truck had dumped willy-
      nilly on the driveway.
I could go nowhere—the car blocked in by the pile—until I moved
      the wood around back
And stacked it up along the six-foot high concrete foundation. Back
      and forth. Dusk, darker, then late.
Back then, I had a pure and righteous anger that stoked the four
      furnaces of my heart.
Back then, I had a pure and righteous anger that stoked the four
      furnaces of my heart.

Sometimes I would stop off at the tool and die shop, or the glassworks,
      or the fireworks warehouse
To see if anyone wanted to go out for a beer or sometimes we'd just
      grab a twelve-pack and sit
On the tracks above the Missouri, talking and not talking as the worn
      day gave way to night's blunt edge.

Home from college. Summer work. Not at home in these jobs. Not in
     the houses where we grew up.
Everything had stayed the same in our absence. No difference. Yet
     each of us now a debtor, a trespasser.

O Exhausted Spirit, Brooding Father, Distant Mother, take me to the
     river and I will cross it.
Take me to where the river is wide and deep and I will cross over.
You can hide from your elders but you can't from God, Blind Willie
     Johnson sings,
Can't nobody hide from God. (Year after year I wait to be found, to
     be found out). *Can't nobody hide.*
*Can't nobody hide, can't nobody hide, can't nobody hide, can't nobody
     hide from God.*

VOLATILE SPIRITS

The day I'll die I'll know, if I know it at all, only posthumously, a
        moment too late.
So I live as if I will live this whole life, the whole of this light sentence.
As always, something will go awry and the shrine I built with
        travertine
And imperial porphyry will collapse under it own weight.
                                        To become
        ash
Is all I ask: ash among ash, ash among the ash of drafts and fragments.

I want to wake and find myself awake amid the fog, Venice veiled in
        drizzle.
I want to sleep so that I might wake to muted bells and the water's
        echoed slosh.
I don't want to lament the duration nor the flux of hours as they're
        spent.
I drop a coin into the poor-box,
                                another coin to illumine the fresco.
I stand in the light until the light clicks off, then fumble for another
        coin.

The needle bounces down onto the record, slips a little asthmatic
        shuffle, then the song starts.
My ear is not tuned finely enough to hear, above the scratch and static,
        celestial music.
I can follow the slide's slight touch, can feel in my own voice

The singer's gravelly man-of-sorrow weight:

I asked for water, but
she gave me gasoline.
I asked her for water but she gave me gasoline.

A friend says I would worship anything, that *worshipfulness* is my
    malady,
A malady and not a balm. If so, then silence is a vow I might
    consider.
For now, I make a prayer to the blur-through-the-trees that is the fox,
To the long drawn orbit of Pluto,
                to the mountain laurel,
To the bracken well, to the whole heavenly host of volatile spirits.

II.

PREVIOUS FINDINGS

Even at night the sky was too large to map, still we found a place to
      rest in your twin bed.
When we went out for a drink in Oxford, Iowa,
                                                we walked past the
      Alibi
And around the corner to Mary and Eldon's Bar, then walking home
      at midnight
We looked to the blurred pyramids of corn by the tracks, the tiny
      stitches of Orion's belt,
The one streetlight reflected on a neighbor's snow shovel, left out all
      year, to find our way back.

I take liberties with the truth toward accuracy, toward the experience of,
Rather than the description of the field of view.
                                     I measure the validity of
      each thesis
By the catenary curve of kite string snagged between the holly and
      Bradford pear.
Given a form one works against it within it. I cannot unknot the dream-
      logic to cross over.
The sheaves lean in upon themselves, a makeshift windbreak, but no
      shelter.

Between the pathway's stones, the scent of thyme—dusty, dry as quartz
      crushed—
Is kicked up by your daily coming and going.
                                     Sometimes when you
      go away

The crickets' clipped songs of ache and ache ring wrong.
I drop two equal objects from a height, but fail to replicate all
        previous findings.
I wait for order and form to encroach. To quicken.

There, along the fire-path through the woods, I was your apprentice.
The past is not archaic, not obsolete,
                        but built and rebuilt like a wall
        of fieldstones,
The present moment frost-heave enough to dislodge one stone; then
        others topple.
You named for me the Christmas fern, the raccoon scat, the hemlocks,
        the cold brook.
The fire-scarred scruff, the elements of emptiness, the calendar of
        thaws.

HIMSELF

He liked to be of service, quick to run an errand, replace a shed door,
    offer advice when asked.
He said *Yes, Sir,* and *No, Mam.* To be excused he asked to be excused.
    He was never tardy.
He had a keen sense of smell and could detect the kinship between
    birch bark and tooled leather,
Tornado weather and the musty depths of a hope chest, the basement
    dark and the dark of a tarp.
He was, as they say, eager to please. He held the door open so long for
    others he was almost late once.

Inside his body he sensed, not a soul, not an airy spirit, but an older
    body mirroring his each gesture.
At a table set with roses, roast lamb, potatoes and rosemary, field
    greens, and wine,
He spoke little, took one small bite at a time and chewed
Until what he finally swallowed was bland, substanceless, and he had
    to admit, unsavory.
Was it his own or that other's stomach grumbling? Either way he
    apologized for them both.

For him, memory surfaces, if it surfaces at all, sluggishly, and even
    then, he cannot distinguish
Between what he remembers and what it is he fabricated from spider
    silk and sawdust.
It is just as easy to imagine the great catch as it is to drop a stick of
    dynamite overboard.

He remembers the sound his father could make with a leather belt,
    folded then snapped.
Spider silk and sawdust. Turpentine and spit for glue.

He liked the zest of a lemon. The other body inside him preferred
    fenugreek.
Sometimes he liked to trick himself—that is, this other one within—
    by turning around and around
Until dizziness set the room to spinning and the house off in an
    opposite revolution.
He made promises, deals with himself, arrangements he could not
    keep. Still, he signed his name.
He stood by his word. He liked the zest—the thin, porous flesh—of
    a lemon.

A BIT OF GOLD LEAF

The day of judgement came and went and still the sun rose on the
      dragonflies,
Their traceries' sheen, the needle and silver thread of their
      iridescence.
The day of judgement came and went.
                                    I must have missed it as I
      watched the dragonflies' backstitch,
The way they bound the air above the marsh's wind-shifted grasses,
Above the sandy bank of Cold Spring Brook as one became three,
      three became seven, seven became thirteen.

I like to imagine the absent objects the hands held, or the hands
      themselves, the mudra of this and that,
The object or gesture that revealed the essential.
                                  I overhear in a
      museum cafe from the table next to mine
A mother ask her grown son out of nowhere, "Have you ever hated
      me?"
The spoon lifted from his parsnip soup stalled midway between the
      bowl and his open mouth.
"Oh mother," he complained, "whatever answer I might offer to that
      would have to be a lie."

Everything I put up in the attic I should throw away now, because
      what I crick my back and neck for,
Pushing an overfull box of old receipts, ledgers, tax returns, bank and
      credit card statements,

Will have to be hauled down and thrown out.
                                      I stand on my tiptoes
              and pull the thin rope which pulls
The trapdoor down, which unfolds down as a ladder—*a stairway to
        heaven* it's called.
With the box balanced on my shoulder at the top of the narrow stairs,
        I pull a string but the bulb is burned out.

A bit of gold leaf drifted down as the janitor dusted the icon and he
        watched as the scrap swung on the air,
Hovered, then lifted, spun, (the furnace blowers having kicked on),
                                                              fell,
        only to swoop up again,
Glinting, disappearing, white then gold, the size of a torn postage
        stamp.
He stood still and watched it dance over his head, and when it reached
        the door and turned out of sight,
He turned to see me watching, and shrugged, first bewildered, then he
        broke into a smile.

INERTIA

The whole hilltop is a concave lens designed to focus the sun
      wherever I am,
Because wherever one is, one is, at least, the center of one's own
      discomforts and complaint.
Never mind the mineral-laden water from the Etruscan well,
The dry southern wind weighted with brine, honeysuckle, and
      orange blossom.
                  No balm soothes,
No mother-of-pearl lacquers the gritty irritant I brought with me to
      Arcadia.

Say, for instance, the stark exposure and awkward pose of this
      woman, naked, caught as light,
As shadow, this woman now long dead, looking into the future from
      this scratched daguerreotype,
With her legs spread and her loosed hair covering one breast, her
      hand cupping the other,
Were meant for my gaze, my appropriation, my consumption,
                          would
      it matter that even then
What she felt was not erotic, but fatigue as the chair arms dug into
      her calves?

As if performing a sign for *whittling,* we said, *shame, shame on you,*
We knew the efficacy of the curse coursed through the interface of
      gesture and words.

We were children and knew the magic children know: If we held our
      breath,
The clock would stop; if we stared long enough at the substitute,
                                           she
      would turn to the chalkboard,
Take a deep breath and then she is sobbing—we made her sob—
      and nothing we can say can stop her.

I wondered why they left him strapped up like that on the cross, his
      fingers clenched around the nails.
The undertow of anesthesia I am climbing out of makes the crucifix
      on the wall
Appear close enough to touch: the gash in his side, the tilted crown of
      thorns, the lash marks,
The single spike pinning down his feet.
                             I wanted to grab it to pull
      myself up,
But the sheets are tucked tight around me and the stitches down my
      belly have me, for now, tied down.

ANNIVERSARIES

Where it narrows, the tidal creek runs fast, then fans out wide
      beyond its final turn, runnels
Branching, tangling, and where it meets the incoming water, the
      half-hearted waves of the Sound,
It ripples and splashes, and when the wave withdraws, it spreads thin
      over the gravel of crushed shells—
The black sheen of mussels, the oyster's flat white, the oyster's
      luster—
And sometimes I wake, look out and watch you there, alone, at home
      amid the changes.

Grain by grain the sand gathers at the base of the dune grass, salt
      rose, and beach peas.
In the sandy low-tide marl, a thousand snails leave behind an
      indecipherable and thus holy scripture.
For seventeen years, we have returned and watched the swans and
      cygnets wind down the tidal creek.
Followed the shadow of the cedar, the osprey's ellipse out and back,
      the carnival spotlights trace the sky.
At the base of the dune grass, salt rose, and beach pea, grain by grain
      the sand gathers.

Sheer in the shallows, and above the provinces of the depths, warped,
      bluish, opaque,
The water is itself a surface of mimicries, a wayward body, a vatic,
      cataracted eye

That sees the fractures, the gloaming, the nuanced stillness of the
     egret, the silt storm
The green crab retreats into, the dredged channel, the raw estuarial
     exchange of spring and salt,
The sky as it drags and dumps its rain all along the Post Road, then
     inland.

We heard the mockingbird as it bobbed on a tassel of marsh grass.
Out beyond the haze of the heather—foil scraps, ribbon, a ring—a
     nest of misplaced things.
In the afternoon, we made love then napped and woke to the wind-
     change, to the tide-turn.
At night, the water rehearsed its declensions. We learned by rote its
     grammar, its lexicon.
In hearing the mockingbird (the swallow-of, the gull-of, the wren-of)
     we heard the mockingbird.

PASSAGE

What I caught out of the corner of my eye might have been a vision,
    had I been a visionary.
In my idleness, I imagine the universe the size of a thimble, the whole
    condensed, a drop of dew,
A plasma so packed that nothing escapes, no heat, no light. It is cool
    to the touch.
Poured into my palm, it rolls about like mercury, but will not divide.
    Had I been a visionary,
I might have caught out of the corner of my eye the invention of time
    and its back-draft.

Nothing is lost, we are asked to believe, not the three horses that
    came to the fence for apples,
The Appaloosa, the sorrel, and the chestnut, that came freely and fed
    from our hands;
Not the delirious flight of the bottle-rocket that set the bramble
    hedge ablaze;
Not the hand drawn back to strike but then held motionless as if by
    an angel, as if by mercy;
Not the half-life of the half-life of the half-life of the half-life graphed
    as an involuting spiral.

I stepped out of the fabric of time, but only for a moment, for a
    minute or two.
I stepped out of the fabric of time and my foot slipped on the last
    rung of the *scala mystica*.

On my way down, I forgot the cause, the form, the matter, and at last,
 the sphere of elements.
I had to relearn the names of the nettle, the thistle, the fire thorn and
 the bindweed.
I had to relearn to climb. To put one hand on a rung, then one foot . . .

Although it is midwinter, a housefly arisen, it seems, from nowhere,
 settles then dashes,
Ricochets off the window glass, retries, then rests on the sill, only to
 recommence.
In my idleness, I imagine the universe the size of a thimble, the whole
 condensed, a drop of dew.
In my idleness, I imagine the fly might one day discover a way
 through the glass,
And the miracle will not be the other side, but the constancy, the
 liquid simplicity of the passage.

LESSONS FROM ART

The gods long to be animals, to hunger and thirst like animals, thus
     they are love-mad,
And crave a flesh that tears and opens, a flesh that comforts and rots;
They believe that jealousy is passion and passion rapture and rapture
     innocence.
They believe we do not see them,
                                that what we see is a cloud or a bull
Or a rain of coins, dropped, dancing on the tile-work, gold edges
     flashing late light hypnotically.

John Ruskin, the story goes, was horrified, repulsed, and confused to
     find,
When his wife first stood naked before him, hair where he had
     expected to see porcelain smoothness
In the declivity where her thighs came together, for what he knew he
     knew from art,
And this new world before him was monstrous, feral,
                            too much like
     his own body.
It takes little imagination to go from there: compromise or aloofness,
     her sameness refused or fetishized.

To give shape to the flesh, one needs ox gall and oak gall, steeping
     vats of tannins to stain.
To give shape to the flesh, one needs silver nitrate, a tea of dogwood
     blossom, turmeric.

One needs a paste of moth-dust, an encaustic of wax and sumac, a
    varnish of tears.
One needs essential oils, a mud poultice, mustard seed, and spit.
                                                                    To
    give shape to the flesh,
One needs to breathe deep then blow into an opening and inspire a
    shape.

Don Giovanni—honey-mouthed, eloquent, seemingly indifferent,
    yet always attentive—
Could slow his own heart, so that what might look like fever,
    agitation, panic, unrestrained anger
In another man, looked like harmless indolence, a boyish calm across
    his bearded face.
If he had to use his backhand, or hold a wrist down, or bolt the door,
                                                                    his
    heart did not betray him.
With the subtlety of a bull walrus herding its harem, he made his will
    known.

FOUR WALLS AND A ROOF

If only I were fluent in another language, I might be fluent at last and
at least in this one.
When I hear an angel rustle in the matrix of vines and hedges amid a
thousand thorn spurs,
When the screw-head is stripped and no tool I own can turn it,
When I find a pale blue egg fallen, unbroken, in the green shade of
the shriveled irises,
It is my own wordlessness by which I set down the moment and its
abracadabra.

Underfoot, the ground gives way to what was a yellow jackets' nest,
but it is winter,
And what might have been five months ago sorties of stings is merely,
it turns out, a twisted ankle.
Through a trapdoor, Jesus, having harrowed hell,
pulls Adam up by
the forearm onto stage.
There were times, when I lived on the karst topography of Missouri,
after heavy spring rains,
The roof of a cave gave way and a sinkhole opened swallowing a
house, a Black Angus or two.

I put a single poppy seed inside a mason jar, screw on the top, and call
it *Lethe*.
I put a single pomegranate seed inside a mason jar, screw on the top,
and call it *Persephone*.

Soon enough four walls are lined with shelved jars— one with a
    spindle in it, one with snake skin . . .
And those who enter the gallery praise the *idea* of the project. Not one
Attends to craft, how not a lid is mis-threaded, how the shelves are
    level, the nails countersunk.

Lost in the woods, not acquainted with the sublime, not stumbling
    upon it by journey's end,
I found no clues of East or North in the snow clouds ferried on the
    wind. No sun, no stars,
Not a single landmark visible through the pines,
                                        through the twelve
    acres of oak,
The principalities of the screech owl, no other footprint in the vole's
    leaf litter.
I was lost, not predator, not prey, but I am here and so I conclude I
    found my way.

A TOKEN OR TWO

To hedge his bets, he would build a temple to the unknown god—
    the one unworshipped all those years,
The one whom he had not even imagined, perhaps a jealous one, a
    wrathful one, one left in the cold
Inadvertently.
        If the brevity of a human life is, as the Psalmist says, a
    handbreadth
And if he knew how easily his own hand had turned over in anger,
    frustration, and vengeance,
It was not too soon to break ground, to clear the forest, to sink the
    pilings, to build first the outer wall.

I never would have expected to see the damp, green hay begin to
    smolder, to consume itself,
Flames, at first, green, more smoke than flames, as if an ink of soot,
    oil, and gum of balsam,
To burn as it inscribed the rolled bales into its ledger, not as an image,
    but as an inventory,
Stock against the future, and then the paper itself is char.
                    The herd,
    unperturbed, stood
Bunched together chewing the late spring grass, chewing the chewed,
    until the dog brought them in.

He built the outer wall from a ruined Corinthian colonnade and
    filled in the gaps with coral and rubies.
A narthex of sardius, topaz, and carbuncle. A nave of emerald, agate,
    and amethyst. Through the gate

Of a single pearl,
                  an altar of sapphire, diamond, jasper, and beryl onyx.
He prepared the altar with offerings of macerated musk, civet, and
        butter, a sheaf of barley,
A token or two he had managed to steal, when all the gods were
        nameless, from a magpie's nest.

I am kin to the crow, cousin to the fire, which tells you even less than I
        previously let on.
I and *he* are not the same, but like the fire and crow are bound by a
        tangle of blood,
Or so I say, preferring to see design in the random, preferring to
        design the random,
As my father must have, retelling a story as if we had never heard it.
                                            He

        forgets himself,
And the one ruined crop becomes the fall of a dynasty, and thus he is
        cast out, a prince without a land.

THE REAL AND THE MIRAGE

At twilight, from our window, we could watch the Duomo turn from
      gold to lead
As the evening breezes banked the radiant heat of the afternoon,
As all that was molten melded,
                                 cooled and formed the night sky
      above Santo Spirito.
I could taste on your tongue the wine's tannin and sweet.
I can say now I was never hungrier nor had I ever consumed with
      such relish.

That night in 1959, I tumbled into the world; the late winter sky
      stretched above like a gash,
A furrow sown with sleet and salt, and not a single crystal stood as a
      cipher for my name.
To desire is to be born without a star, is to be misaligned.
My heart grew drunk and gorged on the air of my own lungs.
                                    No one
      remembers moments like that,
But to begin the epic we need to know what arrangement in the
      heavens led to a hero's wandering.

Despite what you think, there is no silence on an iceberg: the
      windward side ticks
And the concavities, snow-filled or not, bend the rims of notes,
Notes that divide like light through a prism.
                              The iceberg's transient
      form—asymmetrical,

A mutable conundrum— churns up a drone from its pewter depths—
A thrum of water, a creak of fissures—a drone around which a raga
    unfurls.

If, as John Clare says, the place we occupy seems all the world, I can
        be thankful for my myopia,
For these bad eyes that deform edges, that make of the horizon an
        inchoate muddle drawn long,
The trees amorphous, afloat in the fog of their own greenness,
        unstable like heat-blemished air,
The real and the mirage no different.
                                The place I occupy is a seeming,
And even with my glasses on, I see beyond my looking, and look,
        uncertain of what I see.

III.

HEMMING AND HAWING

We were not allowed, for some reason, to take notes, we being the
    good citizens we were,
Having waited half the day for a case, another half being whittled
    down to the deliberative twelve
Who would in the end try to make of the conflicting arguments a
    reasonable narrative,
A sequence of cause and effect,
                        and from that agree upon the telling
    and our judgment of it,
Yet, unfamiliar with the oral tradition, we could hardly keep straight
    the victim from the accused.

Granted, I live a secret life,
                    tight-rope along the contingencies where
    the arbitrary, the happenstance,
The chance encounter are the variables (for which each hem or haw
    is a kind of solution),
And are, by their nature, variable; however—collated, arranged,
    placed beneath a taxonomy's rubric—
What does not seem inevitable, the exception always somehow part of
    the limited categories
By which I know this from that, the secret I reveal, for instance, and
    the secret I keep?

We were asked to learn poems by heart,
                    which meant to hold them
    in our minds and recite them.
Those of us who could not were asked to stay after and practice:

Whereto with speedy words th' arch-fiend replied; Poor soul, the center of
my sinful earth;
Is there not change of death in paradise? Where are the songs of Spring?
Aye, where are they?
Divine am I inside and out, and make holy whatever I touch or am
touch'd from. . . .

Between the shipwreck and reunion—a reunion of revelations,
unveilings, old grudges set aside—
A stagehand hauls up the airy spirit aided by a lever-work of four
pulleys,
A burden that grew heavier with each rehearsal, as if pulling in an
ever-increasing catch from the depths,
And she would swear that she could fulfill, by now,

the simpler task

of a prompter, feeding lines
To the harnessed idiot held aloft, the idiot who sets the rope to
swinging as he struggles for what next to say.

DOES NOT SUNDER

Yesterday is grainy, thumb-smudged, more than a little out of focus,
      as if a mirror of departures,
As if a spirit house open to the elements—mice in the walls, mud-
      daubers in the eaves.
Nobody's fault but mine, the old song goes.
                                 Nobody's fault but mine.
Between this tract of houses and that: an undeveloped shallow ravine,
      a creek that floods,
Room enough for the singed margins of summer, for a loud verdict in
      the dialect of crows.

"This struggle and hybrid desire," St. Teresa called it, "to have God
      and keep the world too."
If I was not understood—the gibberish I rattled, the voice in my
      head—I can't say I spoke in tongues.
I stepped out of my body of fire and into a world of fire.
                                  Estranged.
      Ill at ease. Unpurged. Alone.
From a low ridge in the woods, when leaves were not yet full on, I
      would watch the drive-in movies—
Silent figures of mote-light, shimmering on the wind-rustled screen. I
      put words in their mouths.

I live with a hunger that satiety does not sunder.
                        Filippo Lippi paints
      the Holy Trinity,
Knowledge, that is, of the Holy Trinity, as three arrows lodged in the
      heart of St. Augustine.

The incidence suggesting each arrow was shot from above, the aim of
     a deadeye dead-on.
Nobody's fault but mine. Nobody's fault but mine.
I found, years later, a whorl of burled hardwood where my arrow, let
     loose, had pierced the sapling.

Not far from the fence was an apple tree, wind-bent, scrawny,
                                                            yet in
     Spring a cricked crown of blossoms,
And by the time school started, a burden of crisp fruit, sweet to the
     tongue, but a clench of tart as I chewed.
I waited at the fence for the mare to come, up over the hill and down,
     to rest her neck on the barbed wire,
And take from my left hand an offered apple and from my right
     hand an offered apple.
For my offering, the horse, in a ancient language of shivers and
     twitches, instructed me in reticence.

THE STORY OF THE HILLS

I am drawn to it: the absence of God in my life as a shark to a falling
    scrawl of distant blood.
The day awaits—a guest book open, the page misdated.
I see no need to check in.
                  The year is never *a* year, but an orrery of
    orbits:
The year of the new year, the year of the floods, the year of a
    lectionary, the year of three blue moons,
Birthdays, death anniversaries, the year that is the Lenten season, the
    year that starts today.

My hands inform on one another: the left's sloth; the right's greed, the
    right's wrath.
The right picks up the first stone; the left, a good-for-nothing, a bony
    pillow at night,
Cannot color between the lines or,
                    for that matter, draw anything
    resembling a line.
The right is the straight man, quick with the double-take; the left
    good for a pratfall.
It looks straight out at the audience, and then up, frozen beneath the
    falling anvil.

I spill my father's ashes onto the table and then my mother's ashes.
    Two unsifted piles.
Nothing to distinguish one pile from the next as one slides into the
    other:

Neither black like paper ash, but each a fine powder strewn with
    gray grit,
                like what the wind stirs up
On a plain bordered by two hills. If someone told us the story of the
    hills,
Of giants who once lived there, we might be lulled to sleep as if to a
    song made only of a refrain.

What I write down and erase, what I write down and scribble
    through, is, in its way, a prelude.
A ragtag overture of rests and repeats, rumors and regrets, obbligatos
    left well enough out.
I have not forgotten the spurs of sleet, the winter's four walls singed
    to a funereal tincture.
The shortest day—ice-split, inert, abridged preface to tomorrow—
                                         seems

    as long as any.
The tops of pines and poplar shoulder the wind that is passing and the
    wind that stays.

AS OF YET

After my parents died, we boxed up their clothes, coats, and shoes,
    scrubbed the walls,
Swept up the dust that had grown thick between the gold shag carpet
    and the hallway baseboards.
Shutting the door to their room firmly, I heard the empty hangers
    rattle and jangle in the open closets
Like a gamelan for a shadow-play, a shadow-play in which the won
    kingdom, long after the siege,
Seems hardly worth the hardships, the years of lack, the treacheries,
    the endless soliloquies and asides.

I love best the next-to-last bite, not the flesh above the green and the
    rind, but the stall, the suspension,
The as-of-yet-not-coming-to-an-end, the hunger not sated, the musk
    melon not yet consumed,
The penultimate's flirtation with finale, one foot on the brake and
    one down hard on the gas.
Once, as I looked at an elaborate *trompe l'oeil*—

                                feast, flowers and
        fruits of four seasons, dew drops—
A house fly lifted off the crooked claw of a cooked pheasant and
    revealed the fly's painted double beneath.

The names of things—Halftide Rock, Long Sand Shoals, Salt Works
    Bay, Sodom Rock—
Are as true as the degrees between North and True North.
The jellyfish, a thousand lamps, flare and dim, flare adrift:

A depth of dream not seen, but looked into, through, a reflection
      translated as transparence.
A thousand lamps among the zones of darkness. The riddle, of
      course, is do they rise or fall?

The gifts one brings—wildflower bouquets, wines, fruits, nuts,
      wheat—add to the overload.
In the cave of the oracle, a sweet air vents from a fissure in the rock—
A surfeit of sulphur and gardenia, the turn of pears from ripe to rot—
And held in the lung, taken in deep and held,
                        induces one to see how
      the oracle sees:
The tesserae of ivory, glass, and gold as the face of God, the mind's
      random firing as prescience.

THE ELEGIST

From muck, loam, and alluvial deposits, I exhumed a thousand and
      one fossils over the years:
The passing and permeable moment fired in the earth's kiln. And
      fired, made fragile.
Fragile yet permanent, re-sown as lime into the coal-black dirt.
                                     Tomorrow
Or what seems likè tomorrow, a child finds my skull intact, and
      admires the useless hinge-work of the jaw.

For the elegist, the rituals of farewell and the operatic spectacle of
      exeunt butter his bread.
He writes for the living. He writes to orient the living toward the dead.
He is a specialist, like a tailor, a ruled tape about his shoulders, his own
      jacket neat on the chairback.
(How uncanny the corpse as it stands up and shows us how the elegant
      cloth falls.)
If asked, if needed, the elegist can measure our lengths and widths with
      a quick and intimate touch.

A bit of a song snags in my mind and, like a cockleburr, is hard to
      shake loose.
I won't quote a word of it, or hum the tune, or you'll be stuck with it
      as well.
I try to work, to follow a single idea to its obvious conclusion, but the
      song encroaches,
Interrupts, adheres, loops, gets its hooks in, yet its refrain must be the
      answer
To a question I might ask, a question I should ask, once I can hear
      myself think.

How could I forget the previous lives—a water strider's ease, a
    bluebottle on the dung,
The hollow song of the whippoorwill resonant in a mockingbird's
    skull—
The exhausting dance of one step forward and three steps back?
Still, as I explain the sense of *déjà vu,* put it into words,
                                  what had
    seemed familiar
Begins to fade like a dream one starts to tell, a dream effaced by the
    very logic of telling.

WORD PROBLEMS

The water, full of light, pulled from the well's depth, spilled in cold
        thick braids.
Saying it so makes it so, at least the saying of it.
I disinterred the moon and wrote on it a table of elements.
I roughed out the dream and its antecedents:
                                the anima of memory,
        the image as remedy.
It was August all summer on the river, in the shallows, in the eddies
        and undercurrents.

They made of the language a sentimental monster of bolts and bits,
Clumsy and inadequate in its given body,
Stitched together fragments, histories, theories, and grammars.
Its beauty, the beauty of made things, a beauty of limitations,
                                        was lost
        on the mob.
The monster finds a kitten. Kills the girl. Apologizes in grunts and
        nuanced groans.

I titled the book, *Lunar Reverie,* and went through one more time
        deleting
The calendar of phases, the moon legends, even the names of the
        months.
I read through the book backwards to see if the thesis held up in
        retrospect.
I edited by the light of the penumbra:
                              a red X through the endnotes.
A question mark on the first page regarding the lack of a preface.

❉

Beneath the rowboat the water (wobbled by wind, a tinny brackish
      green
On the shadow-side; on the other, oscillating among brass, ember,
      isinglass,
Asphalt, and cobalt) as water will, grew murky in the tide-run creek,
      full now and fast,
As the stacked-up clouds pulled apart,
                            letting down obtuse (or were
      they oblique?) angles of light,
As you said, "Look" pointing down in the water. I looked seeing only
      water.

SALVAGED NAILS

The carpenter didn't need an assistant, but hired me, he said, for
    conversation,
Giving me jobs he swore I'd refuse, and when I finished he'd show
    me how to do them right.
For three weeks, on my hands and knees, I sanded two-inch wide
    warped floorboards level.
Each night I sloughed a second skin of sweat and sawdust, washed
    blood from my knuckles.
The nails we used had been salvaged from fires. He claimed the nails
    were lucky.

The fragility of the archaic hums with enigma, as if a weak
    transmitter, a radio that still plays music
The second or two after it's unplugged, the tubes dimming then
    blank, still warm to the touch.
Although my hand hurts, stretched wide as it is, I can make of the
    past, present, and future a chord,
A music not narrative, not dramatic, but auratic, aroused from the
    material, from the tick-tock,
Three notes held, their wavelengths constant, or seemingly so, for a
    second or two.

The hay chaff and dust glint and flicker in the loft-light as I doze and
    laze in the barn's slatted shade.
Concealed by bales, a splintery post, a frayed gray tarp, I wait all
    morning to be found.
Hidden but not sought, I slip out of dream and in. I touch a birthmark
    on the back of my hand

And it flakes off like rust. Then my other hand is stained, as is all else
    I touch. I pass it on like a contagion.
Hidden but not sought, I watch the hay chaff and dust glint and
    flicker in the loft-light.

The carpenter claimed to have invented the reflective billboard
    (that's how he made his first fortune),
Signs covered with palm-size sequins to reflect the passing
    headlights, sequins the wind shimmers,
The words and images alive and dazzling in the midnight of a wheat
    or sunflower field (the now-lost fortune).
His sister-in-law (who had once tried to kill him with a machete)
    had—bless her soul—the cancer.
I was his audience, thus I listened, shared the sandwich-half he
    offered daily.

IN THE PERIPHERY

To look without was to look within, I agreed, but stopped short of
      conceding
That the *out-there* corresponded to the *in-here:* the moon's empty
      socket, the shadow's slag.
The windows will be lighted, not the rooms,
                                   Wallace Stevens writes
      and with that I agree.
Self-portraiture is a mode of self-invention, self-estrangement, the
      making of the familiar other.
"Look," the rebuttal goes, "he contradicts himself and expects you,
      yes *you,* to connect the dots."

To put the charm in operation, I mix red ocher with nut oil and call it
      a blood augury.
I draw a circle to stand within, as if such forethought were
      preemptive:
A scissure to avoid the tearing.
                      I look into the shield's polished surface
      as if I could see
And not be changed, as if I might deflect or denude the beheld,
      degrade its lure,
And not be held accountable for the appropriation, the cost inherent
      in the gaze and its lust.

I did not grieve, but carried grief with me as a virus of ghosts, as a
      counterweight.
Radioactive sludge, a bag of bones: the earth holds nothing

It will not give back.

               I did not grieve and thus was haunted, not daily

But in phases—blackouts, visions, idleness (a serum injected into my
        heart).

I averted my eyes, but in doing so saw what I would not have seen in
        the periphery.

The rhetoric of apophasis (i.e., *I will not mention the head of Medusa*)

Is a silver plate upon which a nest of snakes might be delivered, if one
        could draw a sword,

If one could employ such stealth.

                    Caught, looking back over my
        shoulder,

Neck muscles taut, back strained, frozen rictus around a glottal stop,

I had the look—though I need not mention it—of someone who
        knows he's been caught.

UBI SUNT VARIATIONS

In Venice, I think of Hart Crane, as if his underworld stood
      precariously on makeshift stilts,
Washed over, submerged, the domes and bell towers collapsed,

                                                    the

      bridges collapsed,
The way in, the way out silted shut, the sky an amorphous rainbow
      of black and bilge.
For a drinker, drowning is a common dream. I look down and see an
      atavistic remnant,
A mire of reflections, the wake's fault widen, then slosh around the
      mooring poles.

A *paradiso* of words is but an anthill crushed and conquered, a hole
      open now to winds,
To rain, to the sacred mountain's snow.

                              The sundial of the anthill

      crushed.
Forty days and forty nights pass, forty years as one rubs his eyes to
      focus on that distance.
The clouds gather and pass. The rain clouds. The snow clouds. The
      olive reft of leaves.
The olive leaves spiral up into a pillar of silver and stand guard. The
      wind gathers and is gone.

I can no more disappear, Eugenio Montale writes, *than show myself
      again.*
To that I say *I hear you.*
                      I grant that the self is an intractable construct,

And I allow that the *I* who says *I* speaks to embody itself, sincerely,
As if to tie another knot in the long rope, as if to untwine the mat of
    vines that was a garden.
I can't vanish, can't reappear (another translator has Montale say) yet
    the *I* does so before our eyes.

Above the murmur and hubbub of the courtyard below, a caged
    canary whistles up the day moon.
This is not a moment when one is concerned
                                    with the built-in
    obsolescence of the Futurists.
Each morning a calico stalks the balcony's wrought iron, jabs at the
    cage, but misses,
Stretches and jabs as if during the night the cage had been lowered,
    put, at last, within reach.
A caged canary whistles up the day moon above the murmur and
    hubbub of the courtyard below.

BLACKBERRY BLOSSOM

Bob was in love then. We all were. But Bob newly so. And because of
  love, we admitted to happiness.
And in spite of love—the stories we told all night of love—
Our fucked-up parents, old (now) lost loves,
                                        the inventory of hurts, of
    crushes.
How blind we had been, how stupid not to leave when the door was
    open.
We talked all night on the sandbar. In our canoes at dawn, tired, we
    let the river do the work.

One need not count the fathoms if one can read the diminishing light,
The accumulating cold. Yet seized by reverie, pulled down,
One cannot distinguish figure from ground,
                                        lightning from its
    afterimage, the daughters of memory
From nine drowned valleys, from gnats that hover head-high in
    multiples of nines,
The nine degrees of shadow for which memory is the predicate.

At the end of thought is not memory but the end of thought.
Yet having imagined the end of thought one attempts to recollect the
    negations and embellishments
By which one arrived there.
                          And having arrived, the negations and
    embellishments

By which one might retreat from such terminus, might turn and
      retrace one's steps in back out.
Up ahead the willows bend to the water, as a reader might to a page.

As I listen to Norman Blake play "Blackberry Blossom," I remember
      the river
Spread wide over the meadow, the few fenceposts poking up
      weathered silver,
The company of crows that followed us in.
                                Bob was in love then.
We all were. But Bob newly so. The serpentine smoke from the fire
      he built lazed and lingered,
As had the thin whorls from his oar as he had navigated us out of the
      narrow rapids to calm.

IV.

THE FURTIVE LINE

Therefore, past midnight, the sky let fall its sheaf of arrows.
Therefore, the leaves' pale undersides turned over long before the
     rain fell.
Therefore, I calculated the shortest distance between two points.
Therefore, I explained away the hundred emanations and worshiped
     the one god.
Past midnight, the sky let fall its arrows; the leaves turned over
     foretelling rain.

I'd set out at five-thirty a.m. to drive the forty-five miles of back-
     roads to work
And more often than not, I'd have to stop midway to re-scrape the
     windshield,
Because it is one thing to see the blizzard's flak turn into a black wall
     five feet beyond the headlights,
Another to plunge headlong, blind, as dirty ice blunts the wiper
     blades, as the glass re-freezes.
Half a life later, the road is a dream-road: ice forms on the steering
     wheel, affixes my grip.

At that time, anger was my lodestar. An alloy of anger and shame.
Anger and shame and righteous indignation. A bottle of whiskey. A
     bottle of wine.
Therefore, I would say pointing to causes beyond my own agency as
     the cause.
If I said *I'm sorry,* it was not to take the blame but to keep blame at
     bay.
I'm sorry, I said and say, as if to postpone some final accounting. So
     far I have.

Black ice. An allegory of fortune and virtue. Witch grass. Onion
    grass.
An *in memoriam* of automatic writing. The rhyme of *autumn* and
    woman.
The soul, bound as any matter to gravity, moves from room to room,
A slowly deflating balloon let go that rides the thermal up, the cold
    down.
The hand that drew the furtive line of charcoal that is the deer's
    turned neck on the cave wall.

THE TELL

The moon outlined in kohl, lucent above the lopped limbs, is neither
      premise nor conclusion;
The moon—unbidden, untempered, phosphor—inhabited for the
      moment, tread upon,
Is, up close, grainy ghost images on the black and white TV inside.
                                              If it

      were hoax—the moon landing—
Shadowy pictures beamed from some sound stage, purposefully
      distorted to suggest the cold distance
Between here and that surface, why did I believe I saw something
      moving up there?

My father relearned to use his left arm and leg after his first stroke, to
      speak with a mouth
And tongue that drooped as if numbed by Novocain.
                              At first, I could
      not understand him
But nodded as one might in a foreign country having managed to ask
      for directions
And the kind shopkeeper details (one can only guess) alternate routes
      beyond the little grammar,
The two hundred vocabulary words one has learned for the trip. I tried
      hard not to reveal my ignorance.

We never spoke the same language, but there were times I swore he
      could read my mind.
Perhaps it was nothing.
                  Perhaps some gesture or hesitation, some tell
      that gave me away.

He seemed to know whatever I held in my hand, what my bet would
      be, what cards I'd draw,
But by eleven-thirty, he and his poker buddies would be on their
      sixth or seventh drink,
And I was the strategist, the one who could think clearly (even past
      his bedtime) raking in the pot.

I'll tell you a secret: the moon has nothing to do with it, nor the daze
      at night of daisies beneath the moon,
Nor the milkweed on the chain-link fence, nor the bones of my
      father's face seen through to.
Midnight. I kneel and look into the lit basement
                                through the window-
      well to my father's makeshift office.
He adds the same column of numbers again and again as if the sum
      might change, or error reveal itself.
Again on the adding machine. Then by pencil. If he looked up he'd
      see only his reflection.

THE MANDALA AND THE SQUARE

If all phenomena are empty, why does the underdrawing bleed
    through:
A grid of hand-drawn horizontals, lines thinning to where the brush
    is re-dipped,
The verticals snapped lines, the ink thickest at the point of impact;
    the interstices
And hollows patched with indigo's luster, vermillion from cinnabar,
    the red of lac,
Azurite, malachite, and other cuprous minerals on this orderly model
    of the universe?

I cannot dispel the obstacles. Cannot hear the twilight language
    beyond words. Try as I might.
I cannot step outside this well-fed furnace I call a body. Cannot
    account for the hours.
Cannot reconstruct the sequence of events that was the day-before-
    yesterday.
Cannot confirm my alibi. The long convalescence draws to a close. I
    browse among the ruins.
As I look down, a garter snake slips between the gnarled roots of a
    stump spiked with new growth.

"When I cover the square surface with rectangles, it lightens the
    weight of the square, destroys its power,"
Agnes Martin writes, regarding the hand-drawn grids afloat on her
    six by six canvases.

Yet in the very act of undermining the ideal she reiterates the
　　revelations of its perfection.
How does one give in without giving up when one has mastered the
　　conventions of closure?
"The way of the artist," she says, "is an entirely different way. It is a
　　way of surrender."

I broke a stick of rosemary wood and the resinous aroma—a hint of
　　pine bark,
Even lavender, but more mineral than leaf or bloom—rose and I
　　breathed it in.
The fragrance did not conjure memory, but had about it the essence
　　of the *remembered*.
I sat on the front stoop killing time, almost happy in the warmth of
　　mid-March sun,
Desiring this moment and not the next. Welcoming the next without
　　desire.

THE NARRATION OF RAIN

Rain blows through the pines. Rain rattles water oak leaves. Rain on
      the stone chime.
Rain quick in rivulets and gullies. Rain on the river's broad back.
      Rain amid rain.
Rain fretting the rusty clay. Rain at a slant. Rain every which way but
      down.
Rain overflows the gutters. Rain marbles the picture window. Rain
      slips, stumbles, sluices.
Rain in the corn crib. Rain in the trough. Rain blows through the
      pine.

The crow carries a bauble in its beak—something dully reflective—
And drops it onto the path of leaf mulch ahead, caws once, and
      lumbers up and low
Over the gauze of gnats, where wild blackberry overruns the unused
      train tracks.
I will leave the trinket for another to find.
                            I sidestep the omen. Ignore
      the oracle.
Having learned nothing from Sophocles as I put one foot in front of
      the other.

"Assyrians," the husband said, "are the first to use images to narrate."
(I eavesdrop in museums, a bad habit, I know, but one I prefer not to
      set aside.)
The wife—I have assumed they are married, long married—nods *yes*.

"In archaic art," he says, "human faces are a blank.
                                        Emotion is given
        to the hunted animals."
She furrows her brow and nods *yes*. Dubious. Holding back some
        rebuttal.

I have never heard the nightingale nor beheld the manzanita;
I know nothing of the gods: their tedium, their melancholy, their
        blood's leaden sludge.
But I have made a narration of rain as it blows through the pines, as
        it slips, stumbles, and sluices;
The rain as a scattered body; the rain as shape-shifter; the rain as
        blessing;
The rain on the face of the hunter and on the sorrowful face of the
        prey.

THE SUSPENSION OF DISBELIEF

Spirit—let loose, turned inside-out, confused by the cold air, the
      gusts—
Lifted from my body after its long hibernation and was lost.
It saw the granny smith sapling as a brittle stick above the snow.
It saw the smear and residue of cirrus, the vacant look on my face of
      ecstasy.
It no longer takes the shape of what it had filled;
                                     what-it-had-filled is
      the negative space, now, of what it fills.

What's the use? I can no more read the map and drive than drive
      and re-fold the map.
I could pull over, stop, reconnoiter, to see if I missed the exit or
      turned left when right was right.
But the shoulder is strewn with rags of blown tires, broken glass,
      spent flares,
And the stand of trees up ahead,
                         from here at least, looks familiar,
      and if I am right,
The road doubles back more than once, twisting like a sentence out
      of which one cannot find a way.

One can confabulate such voices, deeper than the ocean trenches,
      antediluvian,
Not written into history: a legion of voices in the hollow of one's own
      skull,
Voices filling in the chinks in the silence, filling in the clutter, the
      diminishing echoes

One gives the name of silence.

                        Yet, each of the *voices,* if there are
        voices, talks out of turn,
Steps on another's lines, fails to suspend, for now, its disbelief in any
        voice but its own.

Most of the lessons of my life have been preceded or followed by a
        smack upside the head.
Having let my guard down, I admit, God blind-sided me and I fell,
        down for the count.
Those ten seconds were like a night of sweet sleep, and still sleepy, I
        stayed down.
When I woke, I wrote hymns to the earth,

                            the earth our common
        grave.
I scribbled revisions in the margins I know, now, I should have kept
        bare.

AXIS MUNDI

A scow carried the last of the night
                                        upriver and in first light
I thought I could read the pitched sheaves of limestone rising from
    the bank to the bluffs.
I thought about how this moment and the next and the next would
    house the past—
Chronicles, grammars, a welt that rises, layers set down one upon the
    last.
What is the survival value, I asked, of suffering? The river, a dragon
    of smoke, stayed mum.

To distort perception, to bend the light a little, as if a skewed view
    presented a more accurate depiction,
I let the sentence unspool faster than it is gathered up, and unspooled,
Or at least not winding back taut, the slack creates a kink and the
    kink a snarl and the snarl a mess,
And as I was saying, the thing-said gets ahead of itself.
                                        Say what you
        mean and mean what you say,
My comp teacher advised, but to this day I know nothing of what I
    mean until I've said it.

From rust to sage to silver,
                            the chameleon moved through the
        terrarium: a slink, a dart,
Tail counter-balancing its sinuous advance, head tilted as if in
    thought,

As if it took thought to orient itself, to foreground nothing and, in
      particular, itself.
It is said that the soul embodied as a lizard can slip from a sleeper's
      mouth,
Wander about for the night and return. The sleeper awake
      remembers the soul's path.

Given a choice, I prefer the jasmine's night bloom over the indefinite
      article.
Good cheer, a single smile, over the ripped sieve of the signifier.
I wring what I can from the cloth, use a long stick for leverage, look
      to Polaris to find my way,
Wrap common straw around the spindle of the *axis mundi.*

                                            That said,

    y is not x,
And perhaps there are other ways to solve for those particular values,
      perhaps better proofs.

EXTRACTS FROM A TREATISE ON FORM

I attempt to make manifest the hidden, and in doing so, attempt to
     not veil the apparent.
Easier said than done. In the painting of the volcano, the gray ash
     plume contends
With the foreground's blossomed spectacle of a bird of paradise
Rendered in botanical objectivity: orange and blue flowers flared on a
     green spathe.
The volcano, as of yet, not erupted. The volcano, in the meantime, a
     backdrop for the exotic.

Although it is late March, I stand puzzled by an autumnal nexus.
I translate desire as its surrogate, the object.
I reduce today and yesterday to salt cantos,
Their order for now orderly, ordinary, as if ordained.
But what is preserved? The austerities, perhaps? The rain-weathered
     remnants?

The stations of the cross, the implements of the passion, the wounds;
The five ambrosias, the five illuminations, the eight petals of the
     lotus, the eight perils,
Or, say, the seven hills, the seven rivers, the seven manifestations of
     fog:
I put down a hash mark for each, not knowing what to count and
     what not to count:
One tooth, two quinces, three amulets, four compass points, five
     retorts.

I attend to the preliminary maneuvers of wind in the juniper,
To how the leaf-dust funnels up off the asphalt and resettles,
To how the hawk rides updrafts, banks, patrols the borders of wood's
      edge and creek bank,
As if the part could stand for the whole and the whole for the part,
As if the world before my eyes were merely the *seen* mediated by the
      act of seeing.

SIENESE VARIATIONS

With candor, the devil (silhouetted, visage effaced, torso highlighted
    with crisscross scratches
As if someone had tried to rid the world of this image of evil with an
    icepick)
Points down from the height of the temple's crenelation. Jesus
    rebukes the challenge.
Down here, a quorum of pigeons preens and paces between a swath
    of sunlight
And a colonnade of skewed shadows, congregates and lifts—one
    body—subsumed in glare.

The headache keeps me from the apprehension of immanence.
I stand in the shade of battlements, towers, the wall's embrasures,
    heat-stung, dizzy, disoriented.
Through some gift of intuition, perhaps,
                    I know what it is I do not
    know.
I construct an *I* who senses, in the stark Siena noon, God with us,
Among us, in us. By *us* I mean only the *I* and only for that instant.

Inch by inch, a story, although unraveled and ragged at its end,
    continues:
The ether of grief transmutes into tears, the tears into relics, the relics
    back to ether.
I spend the afternoon studying Duccio's depiction of the entry into
    Jerusalem.

Is the look of awe on the faces in the crowd the awe of wonder or the
    awe of dread?
I admit I'd be reading ahead if I said this had the look of a funeral
    procession.

I've been known to stand at a height (in a bell tower, on the catwalk
    circumscribing a cathedral's dome)
And to imagine the stepping out and off, the curve of, the
    acceleration of the fall,
And to imagine the distance of the fall
                                    as three or four seconds of
    calm anonymity,
Three or four seconds without misgivings, retractions, or apologia,
An amplitude of lightness in which, despite evidence to the contrary,
    one seems to levitate.

SMALL CONFESSIONS

A whole flock of waxwings occupied the holly, feasted on the berries,
And as if a single brush stroke, the flock lifted, banked, settled in the
      Bradford pear,
Only to rise, to retrace the curve back to the holly.
                                         Rilke says, "Even
      forgetting
Has a shape in the permanent realm of mutation."
Even, I wonder, the forgetting of the memory of having forgotten?

Wind has its way. A shiver down the line of the night oaks.
The screen door rattled as if someone were testing the latch, as if
      someone might enter.
But it is the wind and finds the gaps in the caulking,
                                 the pane loose in
      its frame.
The wind carries ululations and whispers but does not make them.
It is easy to mistake the transport for the transported, the tremble for
      fear.

It does not matter, I say, but mean *it is not matter,* the thing I start to
      say
Before a word has distilled, before a drop of spirit drips from the
      alembic,
Before the *aleph,* the *omega,* or the *uh,*
                             has crossed my mind, let
      alone my lips.

So if it looks as if I had something to add—the intake of a pre-speech
     breath,
My eyes sidelong, then up, my hand almost raised—it is of no matter.

Grief remains, even if like smoke it was blinding as it rose, only then
     to dissipate.
I wake with soot on my tongue, soot swept by my coming and going
Into the corners, under the sideboard,
                    inside the shelved bowls and
     coffee cups.
One can scrub. One can push a broom all day. One can clean the
     furnace ducts.
The soot is in my lungs, and I can feel its abrasion with this breath
     and the last.

ZERO

The journal is empty. The sketches and plans for the hanging
      gardens left out in the rain.
The opaque overlays the transparent as if a grisaille's fabricated
      depth.
The halcyon days remain only as halation on a negative: light's
      smudge inverted to a black halo.
The quirk of today stands in as an apt version of tomorrow.
Tomorrow, leaves will replace the blossoms: palmate, serrate,
      undulate, lanceolate, and awl-shaped.

Amid the wane and wax of fireflies, one can follow the creek as it
      narrows,
As one might a rumor, back to its source, follow the snaky bends as
      they arch out, collapse back,
To a trickle that soaks a shamble of stones, puddles, pools, and then
      moves on.
After the sun had set, the heat of the day held on: a dank tarp beneath
      which one is only body.
For now, filled, full, over-brimming with all that is not the mind, that
      is not spirit.

In October, it is hard not to read the dualities for all the ampersands
      that hitch them.
For all the ampersands, it is hard to read the many as one:
The fracture and piecemeal of this and this, of that and that as more
      than this and this, that and that.

The apple skin unreels, a single green helix, from the blade.
The flesh radiant, as if a light source, as if a light the light of which is
       sourceless.

As if to hypothesize the zero, the naught and zed of winter, one turns
       to ice-burdened pines
And does not argue with the daily distortions of perception:
The blank sky rubbed out: white on white on white.
Below the inert nothing, a crow pecks at a drift's concavity, scavenges,
Blue in the blue shadows, a momentary shiver of pearled noon across
       its wing.

V.

BODIES OF WATER

The wetland, a petite kingdom of slimes, heather, bracken,
Brackish puddles, pools, and channels,
                               surrounds the hummock's
      dead oak
From which the osprey slings out in an elliptical hunt.
The unreflective surface of the Sound like a ship's deck scoured with
      a holystone.
The far walls of the kingdom's outskirts exhumed and re-interred
      once more by the tides.

For a day or two, the newly hammered nails gleam against the shed's
      unpainted clapboards,
But soon enough, rust blossoms on nailheads,
                                begins its patient work.
That year after the flood, the whole Mississippi valley looked, from
      above, like a stain,
A damp wide brush's long shaky watermark.
The flood plain, even when covered with ice-sheathed stubble, gave
      way underfoot to mire and stink.

The creeks were bodies for dissection, empires I stood astride,
Archives where mosquitoes thrived.
                       The milkweed silk spread like a
      contagion,
And on the surface, the owl-mask of my reflection
Slid into shadow, smeared, elongated, tore around rocks and was lost.
Spring Valley Creek, Hinkson Creek, Old Brickyard Creek: fed now
      by what memory requires.

❋

Above the tree-lined, rain-filled, clay-edged abandoned quarry,
The circle of sky remains immutable,
                                    the gray of its wings pinioned.
Memory, so easily elusive, so porous, holds the sky in place as I let the
        water
Hold me face up, afloat, adrift, alone for now, and if my heart
        staggered a beat or two,
Slowing down to the pace of my mind, calm for once, I confess I took
        it as a sign.

LINES COMPOSED ABOVE THE OCCOQUAN RIVER

The past nags like a deerfly that won't be shooed: I know its sting, its
    aftermark.
Melancholy, which once seemed sweet, turns like last autumn's cider
    to vinegar.
My beard has gone gray, but not my heart. Not yet.
Cold wind. A whetted edge of snow in the air.
Nonetheless, the returning birds bring with them sutras and psalms.

Silence for all its negations and privations remains adequate shelter.
The sun left its mask on the water. The tops of trees blew every
    direction at once.
If I lost a set of keys years ago, then for years I left the door unlocked.
The plaster's hairline crack lengthened and zigzagged down the wall.
Nonetheless, the returning birds bring with them sutras and psalms.

The more I whittle away the *self* the more the heartwood shows.
I point to the litter of curled shavings on the ground. I conceal the thin
    stick in my hands.
A thousand and one words to confirm the null, a thousand more to
    illustrate,
A thousand more to compound the conundrums, a thousand to
    surrender.
Nonetheless, the returning birds bring with them sutras and psalms.

My beard has gone gray, but not my heart. Not yet.
Although melancholy sharpens and turns, I still recall its sweetness.
The wind's fricatives fumble through the undergrowth as a stutter
        that will not give way to a word.
In the hibernal dusk of early spring, I listen as if they will.
I listen to the returning birds. I listen to psalms. To sutras.

OR THORNS COMPOSE SO RICH A CROWN

The greens—kingfisher, fern, cut shoot, mineral—constellate amid
    the understory.
Nicked with new wood, the crab and cherry relinquish the cold for
    the hard knot-work of blossoming.
Wild's ways less a text than ever. A gnarled language abandoned long
    ago. Holy week:
The dead-fall and leaf-fall clutter the path by which one might
    proceed. A far-off dog bark
And the scrupulous whistle of a mourning dove's wings foretell the
    coming travail.

Rain-light, but no rain above the watershed, rain-light giving way to
    night,
Night to a critique of night, propped up on a crutch of twin cedars.
For now, numb to contrition, to a fanfare's affirmation, I attend to the
    critique's hypnosis.
Last year's palm fronds are burned to render this year's ashes,
Ashes by which the marked are cleansed and the cleansed marked.

I stripped back the bark, and the green wood—raw, pierced by my
    thumbnail—smelled of mint,
Of the recollection of mint—faint, crisp, invasive like mint itself
    taking root where it will—
And thus the mint (truly a mere suggestion of a scent) seemed more
    cause than consequence.
Those who expect the miraculous, I've come to learn, find it. Those
    who don't are sometimes surprised.
I sensed other essences—cinder, anise, noon's tin-edge heat—but the
    green wood smelled of mint.

❧

There in the gaps and makeshift rigging of a conjunction—the
    accounting of *and* and *and,*
The narrative of *therefore,* the detour of *however*—is no cure, but
    merely a mind at work,
Saying what it can say within the confines of its strictures, on the
    worn path of its habits.
I cannot corroborate the execution and demise nor the reported
    anomalies at the grave.
Or, I could continue, offer another story made of only the versions'
    contradictions.

EMBERS

Whether a true or false spring, I awaited the promise and premise of
     the moon's rendezvous.
Whether a true or false spring,
                    the well of stars glowed with the blue
     translucence of breast milk.
I spoke with the other voice upon which my voice is carried
That year of the cottonmouth, that year of the mulberry, that year of
     afterimages.
After dark I read by a snare of river-light, by womb-light in a
     dream's anteroom.

Between the rough-cut cliffs and the valley's burnt-off fog, I dwelled
     in the dwelt-in, in the in-dwelling.
The river below split around an island of pin oak and pine, rejoined
     on the other side, continued.
Later, around the bonfire, our host asked us all to write down our
     angers and frustrations and toss them in.
Good guests that we were, we obliged.
                    A year's worth of deadfall, a
     broken chair or two, cordwood
Stacked in a head-high pyramid, blazed and surged; a slack thread of
     embers climbed skyward.

The idiom of the mulberry is the mulberry; the number of embers
     are those one counts and then some.
Add a hundred to be safe.
                 Beneath the mulberry, the sidewalk is
     stained mulberry.

One can watch at dusk the possum, skittish as the dogs begin to bark,
    skulk up from the creek.
One can rub the stingy last light from one's palm like talc.
At night, the mulberry is crowned with the streetlight's yellow gaud.

Good guests that we were, we obliged, jotting down our
    shortcomings, misdeeds, and regrets.
One by one, we wadded the scraps of paper and cast them in as
    instructed.
Some caught fire before touching fire and rose shriveled as they
    burned.
What I shrove and what I kept hidden
                                blurred as I leaned back
    against a tree.
I drowsed and woke and heard the stars a distant engine, as quiet as
    bees dulled by smoke.

THE RIVER AS A RULE

One can follow the river there through a stillborn backwater and its
      maze of drowned pines,
Through mud pools and cattails, shadow-freight and umbrage,
Along the natural levee that holds back the oxbow,
                              and find the drift,
      nudge, and meander
Of the water within its mutable banks map enough for the journey.
One can follow the river from here to there, but it is the long way, the
      fool's way.

The ever-suspended approach, the sundry quandaries, and the
      disputed anamnesis,
Return me to the zero-point of the mind, a not-so-still point that
      neither abides nor iterates.
On a good day, I might call it *home*.
                      The hundred detours: an *epic*.
      The nostalgia: the *hero*.
Muddy, silt-laden water splits and parts the blue clairvoyance,
Sets down grain by grain the foundation of the kingdom from which
      I am kept.

The flat, copper-green of the reservoir pewters as the wind turns.
The eddies and wakes flash as filaments and traceries of late
      afternoon sun.
I admit my ignorance about life-everlasting,
                      finding myself in the
      here and not-here of waking.

Which is to say, I know next-to-nothing and *nothing* is the end of my
peregrinations.
Above, an iridescent black beetle has made lace of the new leaves and
lace of the old.

In time, sand and gravel fill in the cut bank; flood gives way to
drought.
With Van Morrison singing "Crazy Love" on the car radio, I can only
wait.
She gives me love, love, love, love, crazy love.

                              The road follows the
river.
The river, as a rule, the path of least resistance, the way it made for
itself.
All in good time. The body and undercarriage will rust and crumble.
All in good time.

THE INVITATION

"Just As I Am" played during the invitation and the preacher invited
    us to the kingdom of God.
I admit I walked down the aisle, admit that the past fell from me in
    strands and scraps like snake's skin.
I admit molten silver coursed through my body where, a second
    before, blood had.
I admit I waited as long as I could,
                              then walked down the aisle,
    incandescent.
I admit, a second later, blood flowed again: one half rich, the other
    depleted.

Disembodied, yet bodied by memory's shallow tooling, those who are
    lost to me
Reside in a zone of not-sleep that sags from sleep's gravity.
Those who are lost to me no longer answer to their names.
If I resist sleep,
          I can draw them forth as gestural sketches, as unstable
    likenesses.
I would welcome anonymity, knowing full well death is not
    anonymity.

All winter I longed for the beet greens, all spring and most of the
    summer for tomatoes.
There would be no seasons without desire. The clocks would all stop.
Or rather, desire is a force that pulls things into motion.

Whether repelled or attracted,
                              I am moved by what moves me.
I am moved by what moves me to list the things that move me.

Before the invention of memory, there was the moment. Before the
      moment, the moment's prescience.
Alas, the thousand fragrances of the herb garden do not equal a
      single scent;
However, a thousand no-see-ums can be seen now beneath the grape-
      arbor.
Before the moment's prescience . . . ?
                              Your guess is as good as mine.
I remember well the invention of memory: first one relic in a box
      and then one more. And then.

IN SOLUTION

The day was lit through the ruin of an empty wasps' nest.
Still held up a fifth season on the dead tree's head-high forked twigs,
The nest eclipsed the sun,

                            at least from where I stood, for a good
        thirty seconds.
The corona tattering into an oblong around the nest's torn and
        peeling paper.
A half a minute. Then the sun emerged to set behind the wind-
        clattered woods.

A do-over, we called it. A second chance. The first turn not held
        against us.
I admit I was one of those who asked again and again for a do-over.
If you have heard this all before, I apologize for repeating myself.
For repeating my apologies, without acting in a way that would
        suggest I *was* sorry.
A do-over, we called it. Meaning the previous attempt was forgotten.

                                                And

        forgotten, no need to forgive.

From my back porch I watched the falling stars. The traces of fire,
        white, chalky, not curving,
But angling in. A hundred give or take a few. Each its own as it burned
        and extinguished.
And vanished, I thought, like salt in solution. I could not have imagined
        then the pitted knuckle
Of metal some kid miles from me in Shawnee Mission, Kansas might
        find aimlessly digging a hole

Deeper the next day for nothing better to do.

                                        Could not have
        imagined the shovel's bell-note as a star stopped it.

The tree, split by lightning, stood in a crevice of sunlight in the midst
        of the storm.
The slick palm-sized char at the breech sizzled and steamed and
        cooled by the time the clouds closed.
Despite reports to the contrary,
                           I could not hear God in the thunder,
        in the burned leaves.
You have my word for it, which is all I have ever offered, my tithe
        and my troth.
The truth is that a whole hemisphere of the pear tree fell and I had
        half a mind to mention it.

THE NORTH OR SOUTH POLE

If I sever and negate the beholder's presence, what remains is not
    absence.
What remains is a fiction, like the fiction of a point or line as it is
    rendered,
A fiction that eludes and elucidates.
                              Storm-light lulls and umbers.
A muddy hem of rain snags on the escarpment.
And in saying that, I forfeit the naught of the *real* and the *counterfeit*
    cipher.

This particular light—particulate, a drowse of motes and glares—
Illumines the mind as a drowse of motes and glares.
Spent memory, like a sift of debris,
                            accumulates but will not kindle.
I have been known to make of *out-there* a subterfuge so that the
    beholder
Holds only an image of the beheld as one might a useless compass at
    the North or South Pole.

I have made of not-knowing an inamorata and hear in her distant
    voice desire's dialect.
Every now and then, I feel a cramp in the cramped confines of my
    heart.
The blood, like a root in stone, holds tight.
                        I offer my carcass and my
    shadow,

The nag of obsessions, the false image of my own interiority, my own
      entropy.
Ill-defined, she waits in, and is, the distance I cross to behold myself
      beheld.

❈

Out there, storm-light lulls and umbers. In here, a drowse of motes
      and glares.
In here, calendrical notations of the ephemeral, out there, light by
      which I see.
If I sever and negate the beholder's presence,
                            I am never absent from
      the act
Of severance and negation where rain's muddy hem snags on the
      escarpment.
I did not plan it this way, my love. Present when I should make
      myself scarce.

THE FOSSIL RECORD

In the fragile late hour of early spring,
                                        I cannot shake the cold of
     imagination.
It is my habit to answer a question with a question,
Not to avoid the answer, but to get closer to an unapproachable
     answer.
There is no end to errors on this exilic earth,
No end to the fleeting, fragmented memory-ruins upon which a
     vision is engrafted.

The horse twitches one ear. Then the other. The swallows' shadows
     ride the creek line.
The fossil record fails to disclose the prologue, the getting-started,
The stratagem that refuses the frugal lexicon of winter.
The horse twitches one ear. Then again the same ear, as if to shoo the
     wind from the muddy lot.
The inexhaustible wind stirring.
                         Sleeplessly, indifferently,
     democratically, it stirs.

About every other year, I have to saw off the padlock
                                  and buy a new one,
Having forgotten, in the time between, the combination.
But today, the shed door stands open and I have no idea what's become
     of the lock.
What's inside? A couple of broken mowers, three rat traps along the
     wall, a legion of crickets
And some junk the previous owner stored believing someday it
     would come in handy.

Memory is a bolus of sharp-edged bones, matted fur, gristle, and
    buckshot.
I study the indigestible as if from it I might read the days to come, the
    kingdom come.
I study the indigestible as if from it I might piece together an effigy
    and burn the past.
The little spur of the moon scratches the window that looks out over
    the marsh.
By moonlight, I meditate upon the intricate differences
                                        among
    etcetera and etcetera and etcetera.

AMBER HUSK

The shadbush in bloom. The seam of the horizon a pilled fabric of
      haze and distance.
In mud season, the season when the shadbush blooms,
                                               my mind is
      itself a little muddy.
To displace the clutter, I let the shadbush bloom,
I let the wren's chitter and flight weave a nest in my palms,
Hands cupped as one might to drink from a spigot, as one might to
      ask for alms.

If, as Santayana suggests, things lost can be found, and a faith in that
      must endure,
I admit to faith, even when I come up empty-handed with only a
      specter of faith.
To live in one's mind, even in the well-rehearsed asides, or the in-
      casting of reverie, is to live alone.
It is not loneliness or isolation (each is easily remedied) that pricks
      and stings,
But incipience: the lost revealed; the lost glimpsed but not held; the
      lost, as-yet-unrecovered.

When I say the *mind,* I mean an irrepressible form embodying itself
As flux and stasis, each a reiteration of the next, the last undercut by
      the first.
What I mean and what I mean to say are rarely the same,
                                         let alone
      what gets said.

I remember the solace of melancholy: wherever I looked the moon
      shed a little light.
Even at noon, a little light. The moon has a mind of its own, not to be
      mistaken for mine.

Leaf-choked gutters overflow as if a water-clock measuring the
      duration of my distraction,
My momentary retreat between errands.
                                 I wish I could say there are
      cherry blossoms on the inkstone.
I wish my mind were not so like a tidal flat, covered and revealed,
      drowned and reclaimed.
Soon enough, the cicadas will wrap the baling wire of their chirr tight
      around each hour.
Their chirr, at last, a filament's quiver, the light that lights the amber
      husk I have shed.

NOTES & ACKNOWLEDGMENTS

I gratefully acknowledge and thank the editors of the following journals which offered versions of these poems a first audience:

Blackbird: "Sienese Variations"
Center: "Axis Mundi," "Passage"
Denver Quarterly: "Extracts from a Treatise on Form"
Georgia Review: "Or Thorns Compose So Rich a Crown"
Harvard Review: "Word Problems"
The Iowa Review: "The Elegist," "As of Yet"
Lake Effect: "The Suspension of Disbelief"
The Melic Review: "Anniversary," "A Token or Two"
Mid-American Review: "Small Confessions"
The New England Review: "Volatile Spirits," "The Narration of Rain"
New Letters: "Himself," "Previous Findings"
Notre Dame Review: "Does Not Sunder," "The Story of the Hills"
Pleiades: "Four Walls and a Roof," "Hemming and Hawing"
Shenandoah: "A Bit of Gold Leaf," "Inertia"
Sou'wester: "Back-Story," "Lessons from Art"
Slope: "Light By Which I Read," "Owl in the Vineyard," "The Fever and the Dream," "Let Me Rest on that Peaceful Mountain"
Tampa Review: "Blackberry Blossom"

The epigraph is from Eugenio Montale's first collection of poems, *Ossi Di Seppia (Cuttlefish Bones).* The lines translate:

Be happy if the wind inside	*Rejoice when the breeze enters*
the orchard	*the orchard*
carries back the tidal surge	*brings you back the tidal rush*
of life:	*of life:*
here, where the dead web	*here, where dead memories*
of memories sinks under,	*mesh and founder,*
was no garden, but a reliquary.	*was no garden, but a reliquary.*
(trans. Jonathan Galassi)	(trans. William Arrowsmith)